UNKNOWN SOLDIER

ALSO BY SENI SENEVIRATNE

Wild Cinnamon and Winter Skin
The Heart of It

SENI SENEVIRATNE

UNKNOWN SOLDIER

PEEPAL TREE

First published in Great Britain in 2019
Peepal Tree Press Ltd
17 King's Avenue
Leeds LS6 1QS
UK

ISBN 13: 9781845234515

Supported by
ARTS COUNCIL
ENGLAND

ACKNOWLEDGEMENTS AND DEDICATION

Grateful acknowledgement is made to the editors of the following journals and anthologies where some of these poems or versions of them first appeared:

Wretched Strangers (Boiler House Press 2018) *Any Change?* (Strix 2018) *Filigree* (Peepal Tree Press 2018); *Heavenly Bodies, My Dear Watson, Not a Drop, Watch the Birdie, (*Beautiful Dragons Press 2014-2018*); Disonance* (Hesterglock Press 2017); *Poem Magazine, Vol 5 – Women On Brexit* (Routledge 2017)

Thanks as ever to Mimi Khalvati who has encouraged me to pursue this project and for her rigorous feedback, love and support. To my poet-buddy Chloe Balcomb for the shared writing time, feedback and encouragement. To Jeremy Poynting and Hannah Bannister at Peepal Tree for their unfailing belief in my work. To my uncle, Tony Seneviratne, for the family stories. To Kate, Simon, Annie and Lily for being a constant source of love and joy. To Billie Riley for 'that first walk in the woods' and everything that came after – thank you for my writing room and the garden it lives in, for responding to my early drafts with your heart and for being the one who welcomes me home.

This book is dedicated to my father, Christopher Leonard Seneviratne, who served in the Royal Corps of Signals as a wireless operator during the 1939-45 desert war in North Africa and to my mother, Winifred, the woman who waited for him.

CONTENTS

DREAM HOUSE

Then sometimes you'll think of a makeshift shed,
your father's handiwork in tongue and groove,
where girls with grubby faces, eyes rubbed red,
told stories underneath the sloping roof.

You'll think of long grass and the seeds you gathered
pretending it was wheat for bread you'd bake
in your imagined oven. Nothing mattered
except how long the day and how to make

this secret den a special place. Until
the day your father told you of the air-raid
shelter under the concrete floor, how people
hid inside all night and sometimes prayed.

That day he painted *Dream House* on the door.
He never spoke much more about the War.

I

ARMY BASE CAMP, WESTERN DESERT, NORTH AFRICA – MAY 1941

The first soldier sits on the edge of his bed. It is one of ten beds inside the tent. Each bed consists of a thin roll-up mattress on a base made of bamboo sticks latticed together. His uniform is hanging from a hook behind him. He has made a notice board using sticks latticed together and three pencil drawings of a young woman are fixed to it. There is a wooden crate on its side next to his bed with a cup and a notebook on top and a storage tin underneath. He is polishing his army boots. The tent flap is blowing in the wind letting in a cloud of sand and the glare of a midday sun. He keeps polishing, stopping at times to rub the sand from his eyes.

The second soldier enters through the tent flap. He is cradling a camera, hunched over as if to protect it. He walks to his bed, which is opposite the first soldier's. He does not look at the first soldier. He lies down on his bed and holds his camera up to a shaft of light coming through the tent behind him. He blows softly on the lens then closes the concertina back into its box. The first soldier does not look up. He is intent on polishing his boots.

The first soldier finishes cleaning his boots, gets up and places them at the foot of his bed. He rolls up his blanket to make a pillow and lies back on the bed. He turns his head so he can see the pencil drawing of the young woman. He smiles then picks up a notebook from the top of the crate. The notebook is full of poems he has copied out. He turns to the poem, "The Highwayman" by Alfred Noyes. He begins to read aloud but quietly, barely a murmur. He starts with the "road" and the "ribbon of moonlight" and when he reaches the "purple moor", the second soldier looks up.

They make eye contact, the one holding a notebook, the other holding a camera. The first soldier stops reading. The second soldier swings his legs off the bed, stands up and, still cradling his camera, walks over to the first soldier's bed. He stands for a moment looking down at him. They talk about moors and poetry and the language of photos. It is the first of many conversations.

At the end of the war, the first soldier will take out his Kodak 3A

Autograph Junior, a camera with a lens that folds like a concertina inside a box. He will wonder if the second soldier has survived to read the book of poetry he gave him.

*   *   *

The two soldiers emerge from the tent into blazing sunshine and shield their eyes. They are wearing khaki shorts and short-sleeved shirts, long socks and army boots. The first soldier looks comfortable with the heat. The second soldier rubs the back of his neck and shuffles from one foot to the other, scowling at the sun.

They gather stones from around the tent and make a pattern with them on a slope in the sand. The second soldier goes inside the tent and brings out his camera. He takes photos of the stone patterns from all angles, from a distance, from close up. The first soldier watches him and smiles. He lies down next to the stones and poses for the picture. He kneels next to the stones and poses again. Then he leans over and moves the stones around to make words. He writes OHM SWEET OHM in stones because he is a signalman. He frames the words with a square made of stones. They laugh. The first soldier stands with his hands in his pockets, his right leg straight, his left knee bent so that his left foot is at the top corner of the stone frame. He smiles at the second soldier who is taking photos of him.

The first soldier, still laughing, dives inside the tent and brings out his Tommy gun. He stands at the entrance to the tent, his hand on the barrel of the gun, his fist on the safety catch. He is looking down at the gun. He has stopped laughing and looks deep in thought. The second soldier takes a photograph. The first soldier is snapped out of his reverie and looks up laughing again. He poses. Pretends to be a Chicago gangster. The soldier with the camera smiles and takes another photo.

When the war is over, the first soldier will never hold a gun again. He will never talk about the war. He will laugh a lot and take photos with his camera. He will look at these photographs and wonder if the second soldier is laughing somewhere, taking photographs, making patterns with stones.

LOVE OF MY LIFE

If he drops that camera in the sand it's finished.
I'm finished. Up to now Snowball's the only one
I'd let anywhere near it. He's different. Careful.

But Slapper's a whole other thing. Got his name,
after all, from being so slapdash. So how come
I handed over my beauty to his clumsy fingers?

Thing is, Snowball wanted a photo of us two.
"A photo next to the pattern of stones," he said.
OHM SWEET OHM we'd written, on account

of me and him being signalmen. Bit of a laugh
is Snowball. Doesn't mind his nickname either.
We've all got them. Mine's Shorty. No surprises.

It'll show up in the photo how awkward I am,
leaning back on one leg to make myself less lanky.
No doubt I'll be frowning as well, my eyes steeled

on Slapper's big mitts, watching him, all fingers
and thumbs, asking me, "Where do I press, Shorty?"
I can see it wobbling in his hands. If it drops,

I'll kill him. I'd never get the sand out of that lens.
He's got the sun behind him, but the light's too bright.
It'll be a bugger to develop, with Snowball's dark skin

against the pale tent-canvas. We're not framed right.
He'll lop off Snowball's feet and he won't get the full
length of the shadows unless he moves back a bit.

Careful now. Take the bloody shot and let me
get that Kodak safely back in my own hands.
Love of my life that is. The only one these days.

17

TROOPSHIP

i
I noticed Snowball first on the troopship.
He was different to the other lads. Quiet
in some ways. But what a cracking sense

of humour. Timing. He could get
the timing of a joke down to a tee. At first
I fancied I might take him under my wing,

me being all of 28 and him only 23. For all
his good humour, I detected a vulnerable side
to him. Turned out to be me under his wing.

A team-player, if ever I saw one. He'd sign up
for all sorts of contests – chess tournaments,
boxing matches, recitals. Not like me.

ii
Never intended to end up as a signalman –
don't reckon much to all that twitching and
tapping with transmitters and buzzer units.

Through all the wireless operation training
I'd carried a secret hope of wangling a transfer
to Intelligence Corps as an army photographer.

I was sitting on a powder keg of frustration
during that journey, brought on by my bad luck
and I didn't feel much like talking to anyone.

Truth is, I'm a bit of a loner. Happier with
a camera, keeping people on the other side
of my lens. Getting the measure of them.

iii
I watched him from a distance. Envied him
for his good looks and charm, the calm air
he had about him, the way nothing fazed him.

Rough seas and everyone else throwing up over
the side of the ship, he'd sit quietly in a corner
of the deck, nibbling away at the few rations

he'd saved from breakfast, make a joke about
everyone feeding the fishes. When the tipping
and rolling in the mess below was at its worst,

he took his hammock, donned his greatcoat
and balaclava, slept on deck, refusing to spend
"another night in the Black Hole of Calcutta".

iv
I imagined striking up a conversation with him
but couldn't figure out how. Hoped for a billet
in the same unit. A chance to get to know him.

As we pulled into Tawfiq, I took my first shot
of the war. He's looking out towards the docks.
What lay beyond that view, none of us knew.

From where I'm standing and the way the light
falls on him, it makes a silhouette. Be a credit,
that shot, to any army photographer's portfolio.

But I was destined to be a bloody signalman,
not an army photographer. Like it or not,
I was going to have to learn to get on with it.

CONSCRIPT SIGNALLER

Most days I'm resigned to it, the ribbing I get
from the lads with more know-how, for being
a half-baked conscript signaller. An irritation,

no worse than many others in this desert life –
tea minus sugar or fresh milk; water tainted
by salt or petrol; wretched food. At times

I long to be like Snowball. Wireless operation
is his second nature, a seamless process to him.
Next to his No. 19, he looks as if he's part of it.

The transmitters pip and dash their relentless
natter in his headphones and appear as neat,
pencilled words on his notebook's blank page.

Like me on a shoot with my Kodak. The camera's
part of my body, I'm tuned to its shutter speeds,
its aperture settings. Viewfinder's my third eye.

He looks after those wireless sets like his flesh
and blood. Nurtures them through all weathers.
Sandbags piled up on three sides of the makeshift

signalling station – useless when the sand and dust
swirl into every crevice – and no way to escape
the incessant glare out there from dawn 'til dusk,

but Snowball doesn't seem to care. Dons his shorts
and soft army cap, crouches down, lost in his own world.
What I'd give to be doing something I felt so at home with.

BLIGHTY – LAUGHS ITS WAY TO VICTORY

There's usually a copy lying around in the mess tent.
Several weeks' old dependent on deliveries,
full of cartoons and jokes, typically in bad taste

at the expense of the locals. I try nabbing it first
for fear of anything that might offend Snowball.
Funny thing is, he laughs it off. I guess acting like

"one of the boys" saves him from the rough end
of the joke. Makes my job easier. Confiscating
the rag is nigh impossible without causing a riot.

Not everyone's mad keen. Some young 'uns prefer
their books – students before they enlisted and still
got dreams of going home and doing well.

But one chap always fights me for it. Looks older,
battle-weary. A mop of curly hair. A moustache
with an unfortunate resemblance to Hitler's.

Beats me why he keeps it. Bloody-minded nature.
Look at him sideways and he'll pick a fight with you.
So I took a risk today when I caught him on camera.

Could have got my head as well as my Kodak kicked in.
I made it look like I was taking photos of Snowball,
as usual. "Hitler" didn't realise he was in the frame,

not looking at me or the latest *Blighty* he'd swiped,
but staring into the distance. "Bloody hell," I thought,
"you're welcome, mate. Looks like you need a good laugh."

TALKING ABOUT HOME

Maybe it's me asking him about the drawings
of his sweetheart above his bed, telling him
about my dad's photos, my mum's apple pies.

It gets me thinking about his mum and dad.
Since he doesn't look English and he's a chap
you can be straight with, I just blurt out,

"How come you landed up so far away from
where you were born?" Then I see his face.
Before or since, I've never seen the like of this.

Taken portraits from all angles, studied him
in different lights. Never seen the like of it.
Bloody idiot, Shorty, you with your big mouth.

And then I fumble with the catch on my camera
until he speaks, head down. "My mum died of TB.
I was six. They told me she'd gone to heaven.

That last time, if I'd known I'd never see her…"
His voice trails off. I swear he sounds like he's six
not a grown man. "You know what, Shorty," he says,

"I get my eyes from her. Same colour eyes we have."
And I'm looking at them as if for the first time,
even though I've taken so many photos of him.

Not brown at all, like I'd imagined, but a mix of
grey, green, hazel. I'm staring. He looks away.
I mumble something daft like, "Sorry mate,"

wishing I had his way with words. As I back away,
awkward, unsure what to do, I see how he's framed
there at the end of his bed. The shape of his bent body

staring at one open palm, right hand on his forehead.
Light coming through the tent-flap at a perfect angle
falls gently on his face, catches the edge of his hand.

A textbook image. I take the photo in the silence
between us. Feels like a sign of respect. All I can do
in the circumstances, before I back out of the tent.

TRICK PHOTOS

I like to experiment with trick photos. Snowball
is always a willing model. One time I made him
look like two people shaking hands. Took a shot

as he stood, in his soft army cap, hand outstretched.
Then, as he swivelled round, I swopped his army cap
for a fez and stuck my specs on the end of his nose.

Second shot before winding the film. It's strange
how the man in the fez looks like a ghost of him,
a shadow, a part we never normally see.

He kept that fez on for the rest of the day, looked
right at home in it, he did. I made myself a turban
out of a towel and kept that on all day for a laugh.

Next thing someone's handing out the rare treat
of watermelon to quench our thirsts. Snowball
sets up his own version of a trick photo, with me

and him together. It should've looked like a couple
of melon-slice smiles, but the lad I trusted with
my camera mistimed the shot, missed the moment.

SANDSTORM

A still night. I sleep fitfully, tossing and turning,
pushing off the blankets then pulling them back,
stifled under the weight of heat and darkness.

Just before dawn the wind tears at the tent flaps
an unwelcome messenger. I can already taste
grit on my tongue from the sandstorm on its tail.

I reach for my water ration, mindful of the need
to eke it out over the next few days, as the sand
rages against us and our thirsts increase.

My camera's safe enough, wrapped in a shirt, tucked
under everything in the crate by my bed. I drift
back into sleep. Next thing I know it's wake-up call.

Snowball's bed is empty. He's already up and out,
making sure the signals station is well protected
before the full force of the sandstorm hits us.

SEPTEMBER '42

We're camped on the coast, east of El Alamein
heading down to the sea to wash the desert dust
from our aching bodies. I've come to hate sand

down to its very last grain but here, beside the sea
where it best belongs, it feels like less of an enemy.
This abundance of water, every last drop unrationed,

is poured over our heads without a trace of guilt.
The lads strip off, run in shouting, laughing,
messing about like kids at the seaside. I hang back

looking at the light, the way the blues change from
sapphire through to indigo out towards the horizon.
Can I capture it in black and white? As I'm focusing,

Snowball appears in the frame. That familiar smile.
Arms akimbo, tousled hair. Looking happy as Larry,
as if he's just stepped from that Indian ocean of his.

When he sees me take the first shot, he strips off,
rolls half his body in the sand from top to toe,
positions his towel for modesty's sake, poses again.

"Here's a black and white shot for you," he shouts,
right on cue. Next thing everyone's setting up one
mad picture after another until my film runs out.

September '42. There's news of Rommel's advance
as far as El Alamein. But for a few hours on that beach,
we're just a bunch of lads larking about in the sand.

LEAVING

November 1942. "Eighth Army entering Benghazi
for the third time". While I transmit coded messages,
he packs his gear for a posting to the Ceylon Signals.

I've some leave due, so we have one day together,
trawling the bazaars in old Cairo before he sets sail.
We don't get too much attention from the locals,

since Snowball looks enough like one to keep all
would-be guides at bay. I've got my eyes peeled
for landmarks to plot a route through numerous

narrow streets. My heart skips a beat when I turn
a corner and there it is. Ornate Arabic lettering
over the window. The old man in the doorway,

whose smattering of English is enough to make up
for my total lack of Arabic, remembers me, knows
I've come for the Kodak 3A he's saved in the back.

Snowball doesn't say much when I hand it to him,
for all his way with words. Surprises me later, though,
in a second-hand bookshop where he's found a gift –

The Oxford Book of Modern Verse. "Poems chosen
by W. B. Yeats no less," he says. "I think you'll enjoy."
The last I ever saw of him was on deck as he set sail

back down the Suez Canal heading for Colombo.
If I'd had any film in my camera, I'd have taken
one last shot. That smile of his. That smile.

"DESERT CHAR"

Shorty, only one I'd call a friend, keeps himself
to himself during the ritual brew up. Merciless
banter all round as usual (often at my expense),
but I get on well enough with most of the lads.

It's quite an operation. Precious water rations
poured into a brew pot, set on a makeshift fire –
a cut-down petrol can, random holes slashed
for ventilation, petrol-soaked sand in the base.

It does the job. Burns fiercely until the water's
boiling, a couple of handfuls of tea thrown in
then left to mash. Mugs lined up. Tinned milk
and sugar spooned in. Wait. All in good spirits.

Shorty, when I call him over to line up his mug,
has his camera in the other hand. No surprises.
He's framing up the photo, the way he taught me.
Before he sits, he takes the shot, with me in focus.

LOW MOMENTS

Shorty has what he calls his "low moments".
Says he wakes up some mornings with a cloud
on him as suffocating as the dry south winds
that fling sandstorms at us out of the Sahara.

When a letter arrives from his mum I think
that might lift his spirits. But no such luck.
He comes over to me. "Have you seen this?
Look after yourself she says. No idea has she?"

Shorty's given up on prayer, so he's curious
how it keeps my spirits up. "What's your God
have to say about all this?" He's lost his faith
somewhere, though I know he was baptised.

All I can do is pray and hope he'll find his way
in God's good time. Don't think any less of him.
His honesty's a welcome change. Unlike the lads
who say they're Christians and do as they please,

as if being in a war zone gives them licence to sin.
On leave in Cairo, they head for the dingy streets
of the Berka, full of boasts about "doing the rounds",
up dank stairways, to find doors with names like

Sulima, Fifi, Fatima, Leila on them. These men
call them "bints" or "houris". They're young lasses,
someone's daughter, sister. Desperate, no doubt,
for the 20 piastres each knock on the door will bring.

These men don't care, even with wives or sweethearts
at home. No morals. No-one's waiting for Shorty,
but he's not interested. That's the sort of a chap he is.
When the bragging starts, we find an excuse to leave.

WHEN SOMEONE'S GOT YOUR BACK

Shorty's never took to being a signalman.
To me it's second nature and I try to help
but it's a dead loss when his heart's not in it.
Come to think of it, I'm not sure where

his heart is, apart from his beloved Kodak.
There's an air of loneliness about him. Never
a mention of anyone back home. Only once
I tried asking. He clammed up. I left it alone.

The lads talk about him. Poke fun at the care
he takes with his kit: darns his socks if there's
any sign of wear; buttons sewn on as soon as
they come off; patches on gloves and jumpers.

The lads belittle him for it, the way he thinks
they belittle me with all the relentless banter.
I tell him, easier to take it in good spirit, laugh
along with them, keep both our heads down.

Like last night. Corporal gets back from leave
in Cairo telling us he's been to a "wog-barber".
Then it's all eyes on me. Waiting for a reaction.
Shorty makes a move, looking ready to tackle him.

I catch his eye, give a slight shake of my head
and he gets the message. "It's not worth it;
don't let it trouble you," I say later. But I value
his concern. Helps when someone's got your back.

II

FOR MY FATHER

It was a little like –
black water, like lonely, like hungry,

his boyhood. No wonder
he needed something stronger,

something, not bone-like
(though bones are strong), something

before calcium, something
to pull him away, something

other-worldly – a watchful eye
in the clouds, a hand pulling him towards

the old woman she would have been,
were it not for, were it not for –.

Let's say he was a boy and
he walked without a mother.

Like medicine, the years
between. Long enough to dull

the first cut. Door on door
opened and closed but she was

always somewhere else,
as if winnowed to oblivion.

PHOTO ALBUMS

The Kodak 3A, bought second-hand
in one of old Cairo's bazaars, travels

home with him. Two years pass before
the albums begin. They're awash with love.

Mum with her stylish forties hair-do,
new son held up close to her cheek.

Dad in dapper waistcoat, tailored trousers,
holding his first child up to the camera.

Every photo with a caption underneath
and it matters little that people gossip.

These lined, foolscap, hard-backed books
with torn and yellowing pages tell me

the story of the life they made together.
Like the one of my dad in his garden

with three children. I am on his knee,
eight months old, my small face inside

a fluffy bonnet. On one side my sister,
his arm round her and one of his fingers

reaching to touch her hand. My brother
nestled into the crook of his other arm,

which is reaching round so two fingers
can hold onto my arm. He looks intent

on keeping us safe. The caption reads:
Daddy has more than his hands full now!

DEAR DAD

Does this seem odd? This replying to letters
sent, all those years ago, from a troopship?

What with me not due to be born for another
ten years and you dead now, this past thirty.

No matter. I know you, at least, believed in
an afterlife, so I'll hope you are receiving me.

That reference to your trip on the *Orama*
from Ceylon to England twelve years ago

makes me sorry I never asked you more
about that crossing as well as this one.

How optimistic you sound – that familiar
"glass half-full" attitude you always had.

One hundred and forty-eight men squeezed
into cramped mess quarters to eat and sleep,

and you're writing about how the hammock's
comfortable enough for a good night's rest.

It's so typical of you to think of going up on deck
when rough seas made the mess unbearable.

Wrapped up in your greatcoat and balaclava,
did you watch the stars until you fell asleep?

I'll write more soon. This is just a short note
to say, wherever you are, I am thinking of you.

BECAUSE HE LOVED LETTERS

and the opening of them, I gave it to him,
though it seemed to have been always his.

Its handle is carved into the head and wings
of a bateleur eagle, Shona bird of good fortune,

with eyes of bone. A keepsake from the ruins
of Great Zimbabwe where, ten centuries ago,

the Gokemere made towers of rock, climbing
as they built, dropping rope and stone for plumblines.

I'd say the wood is mahogany but for the flash of
honeyed grain on one wing and the very tip of its beak.

It has come back to me now, though it was also
always with me and lives in my blue ceramic pen-jar.

Sometimes I take it out, for the feel of its sharp edge
against my lips, the taste of questions never asked.

MONUMENT

My writing room doors open wide onto
a terrace of York Stone and I'm feeding

the crevices with sedum and pea shingle.
How reminiscent of a monument this is.

It's not merely the slabs of stone, though
they recall the granite of old graveyards,

it's the filling in of gaps, the acceptance
of what's missing in the spaces between.

GRIDLINES

I'm walking along parallel lines
and the Sun, Moon, Star gaps

on your three-by-four grid maps
come to mind. Hauling drums

of cable, you followed stealthy
sappers. Set stations down at

Beam, Rise, Star, Set – opening
channels of communication.

No landmines here. The evening
is heavy. Dusk will come soon.

DREAM

Dug in on the Gazala line, just forward
of Tobruk, I'm twitching the dials on

a buzzer unit, thinking I could pass for
one of your desert rats in my army cap,

and desert boots, khaki shirt and shorts.
Your battered soldier's service book says

you're responsible for its safe custody, but
there's no sign of you. Sand everywhere

and daylight's fading. And I don't know
how to use the stars to plot a route.

THE STARGAZER TELLS HIS STORY

They issue me with Bedouin headgear, chapplies,
goat-skinned coat, an almanac of celestial co-ordinates,
a theodolite to plot the angles, sun compass, a pistol.

They teach me dead reckoning. I'd imagined counting
corpses when I heard it first, not mounting a sundial
on the dashboard of a truck to calculate true north.

Our real allies are the stars. Without them, it's sand
all the way to the horizon. It's how we fix ourselves
at night, stop going round in circles. Astro-fix method.

Because I read the skies, the men tell me their sun signs,
they want distraction, predictions, belief in a future.
What hope can stars bring, now they are enlisted?

FULL MOON

I want to tell you about last night's full moon
and the strange peace I've found reading about

your war. Circles on my map of North Africa mark
the battle sites. I plot the gridlines of minefields,

gaps you'd crawl through with telephone cables.
I can't place you, but no doubt you were under

the full moon (28 May 1942) listening to the rumble
of bombs along the Gazala line. The moon was there

every month, looking down on the catastrophe of war
(as it still does) in places far from this garden where

I listen to the woodpecker and watch the robin fight
the blue tit for a space on the feeder. I am filling in

the details because you never could. Why tell more
than you need? Why bring the war back home?

THE ROAD TO BADULLA

If we had travelled to Badulla, to find the place
where your father was buried in an unmarked grave,

our driver would have stopped to make offerings
at roadside Buddhist shrines and, even though

you always recited the rosary on long car journeys,
his devotion to Buddha might have made you feel

uncomfortable, but neither of us would have spoken
of this any more than you ever spoke about your father,

since a kind of dogged loyalty kept you from telling
the real stories in an attempt to preserve his good name.

So I never heard from you about the gambler who died
on the Badulla Road heading for Colombo, on the day

his horse had won at Nuwara Eliya racecourse, the win
that was set to clear his debts, put things straight at last.

SILENCES

Besieged by his silences, and pages turning
on quiet photographs, I walk in waking woodland,

where I hear no sound from the brambles,
the moss at the base of the birch trees in bud,

the husks of last year's sweet chestnuts, ashes
left to cool in the fire-pit, the beginnings

of bluebells, fungus on a dying branch, biting
insects in the sunlit air, the view over a ridge,

the open wound left in the earth by a fallen tree,
the heartwood inside the split bark. Until

I step on dead branches for the sake of the noise,
the crack of deadwood, the snap underfoot.

Then birdsong – robin, song-thrush, chiff-chaff,
blackcap – and the low buzzing of a hoverfly.

BIRDWATCHER

After nights when rising south winds
have threatened sandstorms,

up at first light, behind the sandbags
tending to his transmitters,

he finds them, holds their corpses
in his cupped palm, names each one

by the colour of its breast, the shape
of its beak, the span of its wing and writes:

"This morning a desert lark, sandy breast
camouflaged, silent beside the sandbags.

A fallen desert sparrow, "moula-moula",
good-luck bird, brings its own bad news.

First sighting of a desert warbler today,
its yellow iris staring from dead eyes.

A desert wheatear drops from the sky,
black face and tail will hover no more."

BLACK REDSTART

What journeys you have made, red-tailed percher,
Old World flycatcher, *Pheonicurus Ochurus*,

since your ancestors diverged three million years ago
and your species tracked the Silk Route across Eurasia.

European incomer, once a rural rock-face dweller,
you've settled here to breed in most unlikely places –

seeking the thermal benefits of such pseudo-cliffs
as cooling towers or concrete parapets, the rubble-rich

feeding sites of restricted areas, for the sake of the two
small summer broods you must raise against all odds.

We find you nesting, not at Minsmere Bird Reserve,
but down the coast, a rare breeding pair in the shadow

of Sizewell A, defying all "No Trespass" signs, surviving
on the edge of this decommissioned power station.

We lie, flat out, binoculars trained on the boundary fence
of a licensed nuclear site, following the metallic warbling

of your song. Watched by security cameras, we watch you,
intent on keeping this one fledgling chick of yours alive.

THE WAY I WATCH BIRDS

Beckoned by the woods and gardens
of Yorkshire, he flies North at twelve,

thrives for eleven years, then flies south
to a desert war. Though dust soon covers

his colours and the rattle of shells drowns
his songs, he adapts to place and season,

comforts himself with the familiar pips
and dashes of a signalman's routines.

Like a bird that carries itself through
endless trials, in the hope that perhaps

it will survive to breed and rear at least
one chick, he prays each night to live.

NIGHT DRIVES

He stands behind his army jeep,
left hand at his waist, right hand

holding the open door. All smiles,
showing off his new high frequency

No. 19 transmitter. He'll be driving
out to the forward lines by nightfall,

thankful for its clear speech in battle,
its ease of operation. What he saw

on those night drives under a full moon,
laying cables by the site of the next battle,

I'll never know. The wheel in his hands
when I knew him, was in his latest new car,

his one extravagance, his proud purchase
(paid for in cash, upgraded every few years),

from his first manual, black Ford Popular
to his last automatic, silver Nissan Micra.

In one hand, he always held a rosary ring
to count the prayers that kept our journey safe.

Driving into the desert, did he carry one
on the finger that tapped out coded signals?

No roads to speak of. Tracks disappearing
in the sand on the journey to the frontline.

RETURNERS

I plant clematis in a new garden
to mark the end of my nomad days

with enough shade for the roots,
enough shelter for the shoots

that cling to the branches
of an old jasmine. Its blossoms,

when they arrive, are a shock
of magenta opening each day.

No chance of clematis in the dust
of the desert where sandstorms

ran rings around him, so he planted
in a new garden, to mark the end

of his rootless days, became one of
the returners who refused to tell.

How could he know a silent killer
stalked him and would arrive later,

like a message from a war zone
with news of a too-early death?

NEVER A WORD

I'm trying to decipher the paperwork from the MOD,
or match the thumbprint in his soldiers service book,

and the story sways away from me – the way he'd sway
with my mum at those dinner dances, in his leather-soled

dancing shoes. He tried to teach me the steps of a waltz
or a foxtrot. Me with my mod haircut, long down one side

over my eyes and two corkscrew curls by my ears.
This digging is exhausting and never a word from him.

What about his memories that went underground and
stay there with the weight of his headstone on them?

THE WEIGHT OF THE WORLD

Oh, how they blew like vast sails in the breeze,
my mother's wet sheets, pegged hard to the rope
of her washing line. There was always hope
of dry weather and no need for a please
or thanks between us as we hauled them down.
Whether to make the fold from right to left
or left to right, to tame the restless heft?
My job to know. I won't call it a dance
but there were steps to learn and cues to read,
the give and take of fabric passed like batons
in a relay race. She was my due north.
Her right hand set west, mine tracing the east,
we closed the distance, calmed the wayward weight,
bringing order to the billowing world.

DEAR MUM

Not a word from you until today. I was pegging out
the washing and it was as if you were there next to me,
reaching to fasten a sheet in loops on my washing line.

You were always a say-it-like-it-is, speak-as-you-find,
no-nonsense – some might call it sharp-tongued –
kind of person, so your silence had surprised me.

And there's no criticism implied. I'm grateful to you
for teaching me to speak my mind and for the cushion
of love, the space for comfort in the crook of your arm.

I've been wondering about your war years, how it felt
to be the one he left behind in 1941 and all the waiting.
You wrote letters, your sister helped you with the spelling.

Not your fault you were taken out of school at 13 to be
the one who helped at home – what with my grandma
having her mother and a sick relative to look out for.

That bout of TB when you were six can't have helped.
Nearly two months alone in a sanitorium, you told me,
no visitors allowed. Looking out for them every day.

Must have been five years before you saw my dad again,
not knowing whether he'd survive. Not to mention
the posting to Ceylon – the worry he'd decide to stay on.

It was a long engagement for sure, but the wedding photo
tells its own story. Head held high, you're looking round
at all the guests as if to say, "See. He was worth the wait!"

I'll write more soon. Glad you came to break the silence.
I can still hear your voice, those broad Yorkshire vowels
asking me, "Why is your dad getting all the attention?"

REMEMBER

that first walk in the woods, fallen leaves
underfoot, turning to mulch on a muddy path,

where I found a berry – rowan, you said –
and if the shell of an acorn was the berry's boat,

the oak leaf was its ocean – all of which became
my offerings left by the archway of a curved branch,

before bending to see the face of a woman carved
by the movement of rock against itself, her brow

leaning against stone, her gaze fixed on an elephant
dancing under a bright fern which had sprouted,

against all odds, from a cleft in the rock. Remember
the broken tree by the pond where you traced the flight

of a kingfisher you once saw, and how I followed
the arc of its blue as if I could see it in your memory?

LEES MOOR WOOD

Forgive us, we trespassed
for the sake of an easier route.

It was the heat, the long grass
stippled with nettles, my body

overreacting to the pollenated air,
too many fences – No Public Access.

What did I expect then? The perfect
interlude for my state of unrest?

Beech trees are normally so reliably
harmonious, but that day, discordant

chimes of bad news were hanging
carelessly from their branches.

Who cares about finding a summit
or plotting numbers in a grid reference?

There's seventy-nine missing
presumed dead and still counting.

And how will we forgive those
who trespassed against them?

THE DEVIL'S ROPE

I

Devil knows I've mauled a good few bodies
in my day and often left the souls for him.
Lock-out? Lock-in? Moot point and makes no odds.
Whatever way you cross, I'll cut your skin
but still you try to dodge my barbs, poor sods.
I've crossed the open plains and closed them in,
I've edged a desert war, I've manned the trenches.
Now I'm raising Fortress Europe's latest fences.

II

A pioneer in 1871,
I was proud to be the settlers' solution.
Who cared if tribal ways of life were gone
now that the buffalo would face extinction.
Don't blame me – a mere pawn in Lincoln's plan
to span from coast to coast and build a nation.
He left the Sioux and Cheyenne with no hope –
I guess that's why they named me "Devil's Rope".

My exploits in the trenches made me famous,
I thrived in war, I stood up to the test.
I'm proud to say my presence made men nervous.
My coils were sharp. Troops fell. You know the rest.
I'll tell you, at the risk of sounding callous,
I served both sides and always did my best
to shield them, but my main aim was to rip.
So countless soldiers died whilst in my grip.

I did the job so well they brought me back
for World War Two. Ideal for desert duty,
on Rommel's frontline against the Desert Rats,
I travelled north from Sollum over thirty
sandy miles to Jaghboub. Hard to keep track
of all my talents, all my dirty tricks.
One thing is clear, I'm keen to serve, upstanding.
To tell the truth, I don't care who's commanding.

I'm not done yet. Now Europe needs defence.
It's not my fault if children get entangled
in my razor wiring. There's no pretence
the work is tough, seen from any angle,
no matter their distress, I am the fence
that holds Europe's borders. Let's not wrangle.
Though refugees might want the chance to settle,
I thwart their hopes – proving the strength of metal.

DOES ANYONE HAVE ANY INFORMATION?

Found poem from entries in "Those known to have served in the Royal Signals"
Wartime Memories Project

He died of cancer, it started at the site of that bullet wound
The MOD needs his army number, which I don't have
He was buried at Heliopolis in the war cemetery
I'm waiting for a copy of his death certificate
He drove over a landmine and was killed
His mother tore her hair out in handfuls
I suspect he may have been captured
Trying to find out what happened
Information greatly appreciated
I'm trying to find out more
He died aged twenty-two
I don't know for sure
He had night terrors
He was captured
He went missing
This is all I know

COBALT

I'd rather be known for my blue notes, cool notes,
my porcelain pigments, my Bohemian heritage.
That's not a goblin you see in my mirror, I'm clean —

a purer tint than Prussian, the painter's friend,
a good substitute for skies where ultramarine fails,
ideal for half-tones in lights, violet shades in flesh.

Don't let the stories you hear tarnish my reputation.
Think how Cézanne, Pisarro and Turner lauded me.
Look at me in that light — atmospheric, unsubstitutable,

essential in any landscape. Did you know, at Lavacourt,
Monet made a field of pure snow from me with only
hints of white? Renoir relied on me and, as for Van Gogh,

his *Starry Night over the Rhone* would be nothing
without my stable smalt. Credit where it's due, I should thank
the colour merchant, Thénard, whose timely intervention

widened my horizons from metallic to more artistic pursuits.
But these days, I'm a victim of my own moderate malleability.
Believe me, it's no choice of mine, this unholy union with nickel.

I'd no desire to join an aristocracy of superalloys, don't care
how high they fly, bent as they are on conquering the skies.
I was the sky. I am the sky. Remember me for that.

SOME MAPS

tell us nothing about the lies
of the land or how straight lines

came to be drawn in places where
once contours marked out borders

so that the land and its people curved
into each other like sleeping lovers.

No maps

to speak of when he gave me
his hands which were turning

grey over the brown, the way
his hair had gone grey and thinner,

the way he got thinner and by then,
I'd given up on wishing for more.

Some borders

tell us nothing about the lives
risking the sea as crossing points

in boats with no lists and no names
for those who've spilled out of them,

desperate enough to sink their savings
to purchase the privilege of drowning.

No borders

to speak of, though his worrying
hands seemed to be tapping out

coded messages from a desert war,
where the forward lines moved

back and forth as if a hand of God
was drawing them in the sand.

LAST VISIT TO THE HOSPICE

I held his hand, it was the only thing to do,
as I swallowed all the words I'd planned
and quenched his quiet thirst with sips of water.

After years of push and pull between us,
his wishes I could never have fulfilled,
I held his hand; it was the only thing to do.

No more disappointments, no more questions,
I travelled with him on the open road to death
and quenched his quiet thirst with sips of water.

The ward TV screen flickered daytime soaps;
I closed my eyes and felt the swoop of swallows;
I held his hand; it was the only thing to do.

He was on the edge of heaven, talking to the dead,
I, the non-believer, stayed there with him
and quenched his quiet thirst with sips of water.

In the end it seems that all I'd ever wanted
was to hold his hand in comfort, so
I held his hand; it was the only thing to do,
and quenched his quiet thirst with sips of water.

AT THE CO-OP FUNERAL DIRECTORS

My brother has the paperwork, I have the pyjamas.
I consider the word "Directors" as if this is a play

to be performed in the days ahead, under the gaze
of these men. We take our seats, trade certificates

for sympathy, submitting to the formal requirements
of dying before returning to the business of grieving.

Yes, he was born on this date, and yes, he died on that
and perhaps pale oak with brass handles for the coffin.

Without the rectangle of pale-green cotton, ironed
and folded, under my resting palms, this would be

no more than a necessary exchange between strangers.
But my mother's words, spoken this morning

as we left the house are waiting in the wings
to be said aloud: "I want him buried in his pyjamas."

WHERE A RIVER MEETS THE SEA

I've been searching in the Laccadive Sea for a story, though
it's not mine to tell. In any case it eludes me, too deeply

submerged for my held breath and I'm not made for sea-diving.
What I need is as fragile as the soft-bodied polyps, busy building

coral reefs to hide in. I scour the stony skeletons, bone-grafting
one story with another. It's no good. I want the journey I never had,

with the old man my father never became. I want to stand at the mouth
of the Kalu Ganga with him, say, "So this is the sea, Dad, this is the sea

that carried you, motherless, over its horizon, so far removed from
monsoons and mangosteens that you learned to live without them.

You were a child migrant. Not like these days, you had safe passage
and a welcome when you arrived. You found love here, taught me

to value what's in the cup more than what's been spilled, how to
gather summer fruits and preserve their joy through winter."

THE HABIT OF HOPE

Though it's sometimes nurtured by the naming of birds,
mine's not "a thing with feathers", but more like measured

footfall on a slow walk to the hide, the moon a crescent
in morning sky, putting one foot in front of another towards

the promise of a stillness, which is more like hovering,
the way a hummingbird hovers, fifty wing-beats per second,

savouring moments of colour, collecting nectar in small sips,
playing a part in the bigger picture of survival. It is after all

what I leaned on, this habit, this year when every month seemed
to bring bad news and I held my breath waiting for results

of one kind or another. You see, my dad taught me years ago:
even when there's no cure in sight, when the pain has invaded

your bones and your leg can't press the clutch, you don't give up,
you swap your manual gears for automatic and keep on driving.

LLEGADA

On the first night I wake up with a start
as if someone has called out to me,

but there's only the moon through
the skylight, silent as ever, bright enough

to make my painted toenails look like stars
in the darkened room. There are too many

lanterns of bad news hanging in my branches
with no need to be named any more than

the creak of the door which, opening, lets me out
and down the steps to where the white knight

is waiting to make a move in a face-off
with the blue bishop on the terrace.

Why can't everything be as dependable
as a lemon tree or the ruined house

across the valley which, just like last time,
looks surprised to see me again.

STATIONS OF THE CROSS – RELLEU, SPAIN

I
I leave my blue lodgings across the valley,
find ciçadas in the evening heat of trees
where *Jesus is sentenced to death* and led away.
Pontius Pilate is washing his hands of it.

II
As I climb the Calvary steps, *Jesus is made
to carry his Cross.* Each station is a scene
on painted tile. Strange how the names
come back to me after all these years.

III
Jesus falls the first time. A crowd surges,
urging him to his feet. Roman soldiers
jab his flesh with sticks. There is a tree
beside me. It is not my father. Yet it is.

IV
I want him to tell me the forgotten name
of this station. I am in a long-ago church,
with smells of incense and candle wax,
asking him, "Who are these women?"

V
Someone helps Jesus to carry the Cross.
The Roman soldiers have been defaced
over the years by the local, unforgiving
faithful. He would have forgiven them.

VI
This one I know. *Veronica wipes the face
of Jesus.* It makes an imprint on her cloth
like an image from my childhood home,
its eyes following me, wherever I went.

VII
We'd be halfway through at this point,
the church too dark to see the pictures,
but my father, knowing them by heart,
would whisper, *"Jesus falls a second time."*

VIII
There's an echo inside each stone shrine.
A baby reaches out. Someone behind me
is complaining about the weeping women
being on their knees. I defend their belief.

IX
Jesus falls a third time. These "falling" scenes
are easier to remember. Watching my father
in those days, the strength of his belief, how
he'd fall to his knees as if he felt the pain of it.

X
There's violence in every scene. This one adds
humiliation as *Jesus is stripped of his garments*
by brutal men. Dried pine needles underfoot.
Lantana flowers that remind me of Sri Lanka.

XI
Jesus is nailed to the Cross. The man who strikes
the nails through his hands is all but obliterated,
the tiles hacked away, the plaster deteriorated.
A sign says INRI. I can't remember what it means.

XII
The cross is raised and *Jesus is crucified*, nailed by
his hands and feet. Mary Magdalene's tears,
Mother Mary's prayers. A child again, I watch
my father bow his head, to weep and pray.

XIII

Mary Magdalene watches as *Jesus is taken down
from the Cross*. Her face has been scratched out.
In the chapel on the hill, I may light candles
and kneel, not in prayer but in memory of his.

XIV

Sunset throws light on the fourteenth station.
Three empty crosses, *Jesus is buried in the tomb*.
The chapel is closed for renovation. I leave
my father on the hill, retrace my steps alone.

NOTES

p. 31: "The Stargazer Tells His Story"
In November 1941, the Long Range Desert Group were assigned to the 8th Army, Desert Rats. They were a reconnaissance and raiding unit of the British Army and experts in desert navigation using the stars to plot their routes.
Chapplies – Desert sandals

p. 44: "Lees Moor Wood"
The fire, which destroyed 24-storey Grenfell Tower on 14 June 2017 was one of the UK's worst modern disasters. A week after the fire there were reports of 79 people still missing and presumed dead. The spread of the fire was largely exacerbated by flammable exterior cladding on the building. It was the worst UK residential fire since the Second World War.

p. 48: "Cobalt"
Cobalt and nickel based superalloys are used to create speciality steel for weapons, military aircraft and drones.

p. 63: "a thing with feathers"
This refers to Emily Dickinson's poem, "'Hope' is the thing with feathers".

III

ALBUM

Photographs taken between 9 May 1941 and 22 November 1942

Port Tawfiq, Egypt
Cairo, Egypt
Jericho, Palestine
Coastal location east of El Alamein
Eighth Army camps in the deserts of Egypt and Libya

Picture in uniform of the Ceylon Defence Force taken in
Colombo between 1943 and 1945

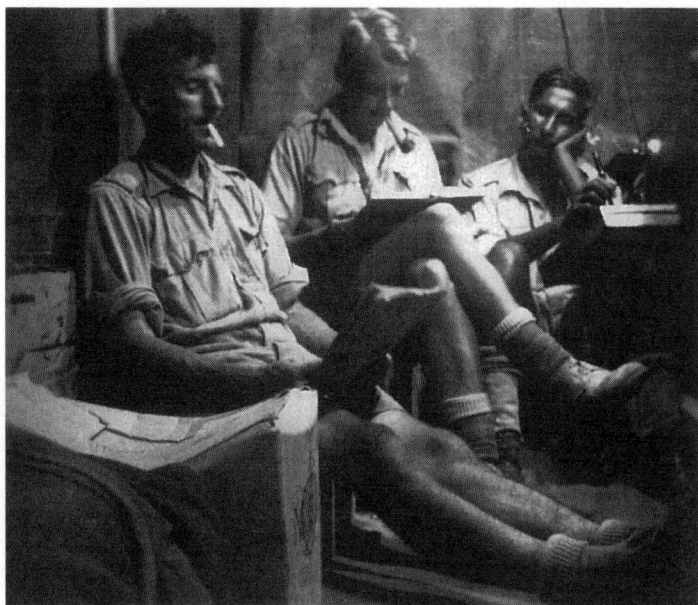

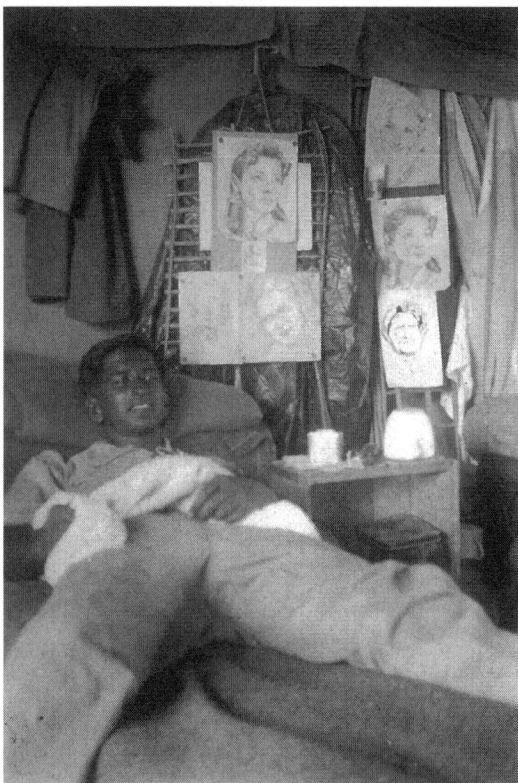

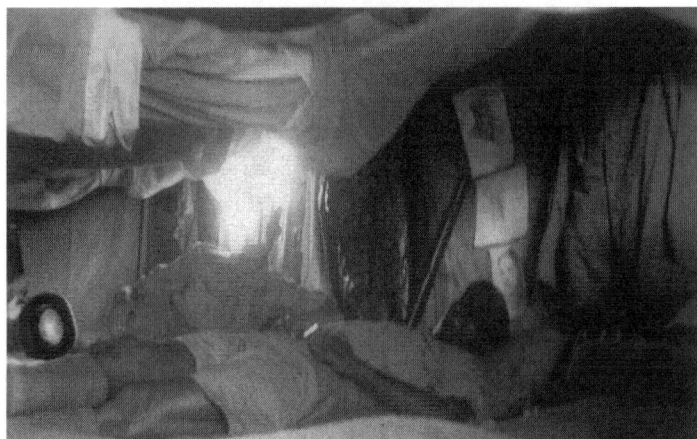

77

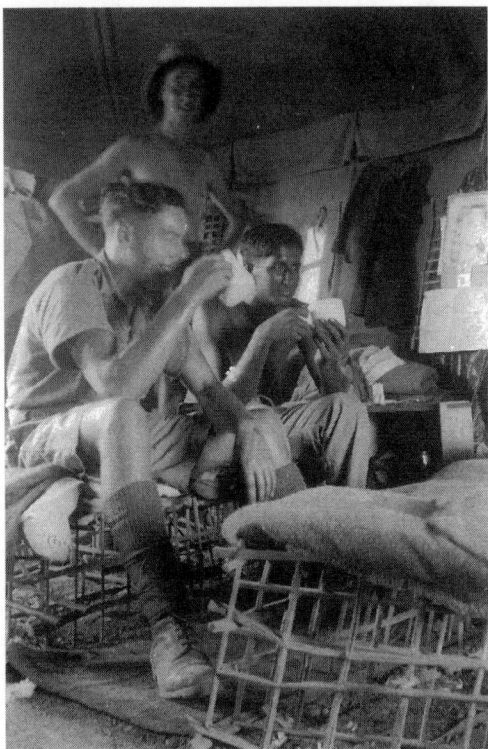

Destination L.

2342118 Sgm Seneviratne. C.L.

R. Signals.

Draft No. 29877.

G.H.Q. 2nd Echelon.

℅ Army P.O. 890.

22nd Mar. 1941.

Dearest Daddy & Mummy,

      As you will have probably heard by the time you get this letter, I am leaving England for Active Service elsewhere, & as you can see by the address my destination is definitely a warm one. I am not as yet able to tell you just where we are going, but it is definitely nearer to you than I am now. I am beginning this letter now, & I am going to continue it during the voyage & post it at the earliest opportunity.

      We came on board the troopship on the Feast of St Joseph & we are now on the move. Everyone crowded along the rails to watch the tugs manoeuvre us out of the Port. There were no friends or relations here to wave us goodbye, & the departure was marked by an absence of fond farewells. But we waved to everybody we could see, & there were plenty of humourous remarks, laughing & singing.

leaking then" meaning, of course, that someone else would be in possession of a leaking mug.

23rd Sunday.

I am reclining at present in the middle of a deck that is bathed in sunshine, & covered with figures dressed in khaki. There is a beautiful blue sky above & we are surrounded by a sea that reminds you of pictures of the Mediterranean. We have a good idea where we are, but Mr Censor might object to my telling you. Suffice it to say that we have now joined our convoy & are moving peaceably towards our destination. We might almost be on a pleasure cruise, if it wasn't for the abundance of khaki & the absence of Eve.

Sunday in a troopship is very little different from any other day. It doesn't seem like Sunday to me with no early mass & communion. As a matter of fact we have no Priest on board. But all the Catholics gathered together this morning & an Officer read us the Gospel & a sermon of St Augustine's & we said a few prayers together. I wonder how long it will be before we see a Church & the Blessed Sacrament. This is going to be the queerest Passiontide & Easter I have ever experienced.

to spend on board.

After a very interesting day, I am now sitting on deck & watching a sunset that can only be seen in the tropics. As the sun slowly descends, so the sky round it changes through a hundred & one shades from yellow, to orange, red mauve & then purple. I had always looked forward to seeing one of there sunsets again, & I ~~have~~ never guessed that it would be in these circumstances. I had always dreamed of a trip back East in an ocean line, but this trip is very much different from all those dreams.

9th Wednesday

We left land day before yesterday, & we are now in the middle of the ocean again. The heat in our mess has been so bad that we have had our meals dressed in P.T shorts & identity discs, & sweat has poured off us like water. Everyone has realised the wisdom of getting his hair cut short, irrespective of what he looks like. Several have had it all off, & there are some really funny sights. You might even have difficulty in recognizing me as my hair is too short to take a parting.

I am sorry to say that the food has deteriorated, & gradually gone from bad to

well & happy, & are not feeling much effect of
this war. Please dont worry too much about
me, because as you can see from this letter, I
am not having such a bad time. I will
continue to write like this whenever I have
anything to say, & post it at the first
available opportunity. I hope they all reach
you & in the proper sequence.

      With love & kisses to Daddy,
Mummy, Belle, Mervyn, Tony & Sena

         I remain

         your affec. son

         Lyn.

P.S.
    I hope you heard my wireless
message.

Destination "L."

234 2118 Sgm Senewiratne Lt.

R. Signals

Draft No 29877.

GHQ. 2nd Echelon

℅ Army P.O. 890.

24th Thurs. Apr. 1941.

Dearest Daddy & Mummy

      I hope you have already received the first instalment of my description of this journey. It was sent off at the Port we have just left & now that we are well under way again I am beginning my second instalment. The chances are that I might not be able to post it until we reach our destination, but as long as you receive it, that is all that matters.

      Before going on to tell you all about our short stay at this South African port, let me mention the success we had in a concert given by a few of our unit. We drew it up ourselves & it consisted of chorus & individual turns lasting an hour & a half. My turn was the reciting of "The Pig-tail of Li Fang Fu." We first gave the show to the ranks & we received a very good reception. It was such a success, that we were invited to give the same show in the Officer's mess. There we received an even greater indication of appreciation, & we felt quite satisfied with our efforts. But that was not all, for we were then invited to repeat the show for the

94

currency we were in — we were very quick to
get ready & leave the boat to which we had
been confined for so many weeks. Unfortunately
the rain was coming down in sheets, & despite
our overcoats we were dripping wet in a very
few minutes. But even that failed to rob us
of the thrill we felt as we left the dock
boundaries & entered into this wonderful city.
The tall white buildings, the straight wide
roads set out symmetrically told us that this
was no city that had sprung up in a night,
but a well-planned & orderly metropolis. We were
struck by the sky-scrapers that were liberally
scattered about, the cleanliness of the streets,
& the populace — white, black & brown — caring
little or nothing for one another. To most chaps, it
was something entirely new — a revelation. But for me,
it was slightly different. Faintly my memory recalled
something like this seen before. Surely this
promenade involuntarily calls to mind the world-
famous face, & where else have I seen rickshaws
but in Colombo. But in spite of the rain I began
to see that this wonderful city was really quite
different from what my memories & dreams told
me of my native Colombo.

　　　　We had promised ourselves that the
first thing we would do on shore would be to
have a good feed. But apparently everybody else had

the welcome that we got at this outpost of the Empire, & we would all like to visit it again under more favourable circumstances.

We are once more on the high seas, & although it was warm enough in South Africa, it seems to be getting hotter every day. Back again to the old routine in the "Queue" ship or the "Hell" ship as it is called, those memorable few days seem something like a dream. Everyone of us has something interesting to tell of his exploits, & the censor is certain to have a good time reading all our accounts.

2nd May 1941.

Yesterday was Mervyn's 21st birthday & this is the only opportunity I have of congratulating him on attaining his majority. Please give him my very best wishes. I hope that he has now turned the corner, & is on his way to a successful career.

Although I have not written for a week my thoughts have been quite a lot with you. As you can imagine we have been in the Indian Ocean, & I realised that somewhere to the East of us lay a little island which contained such a lot that was dear to me. I knew that some time last week we were passing very near to my Native Ceylon compared to what I've been in the last

96

both occasions in grand style, joining hands & singing "Auld Lang Syne" & "God save the King".

The next item is the Chess tournament. I am sorry to say that in the semi-final, just when I was getting the better of my opponent, I made a silly mistake which often proves fatal in Chess – & this time it did. I realised as soon as I'd done it, but it was too late, & my opponent went on to the Final.

I am also enclosing the first edition of our News Letter, which is the product of somebody's brilliant idea. It should supplement this letter of mine as well as serve as a souvenir. It has won the approval of everyone, & you will agree it is a great idea. I feel I must mention however that it contains one sentence with which we are bound to disagree, namely: "Food is very good". What I have said elsewhere about the food is more correct.

Well, I have now reached the end of this part of my story. In two or three days we should be disembarking & then – I wonder what is in store for us. I shall continue to write & tell you all the news that the Censer will permit. I hope that the letters you write direct to me will arrive more regularly than the mail did in England.

In conclusion let me say that we are all in high spirits & every man in this

ABOUT THE AUTHOR

Seni Seneviratne, born and raised in Leeds, is of English and Sri Lankan heritage. She has given readings, performances and workshops in UK, US, Canada, South Africa, Egypt and Kuwait. She currently works as a freelance writer, mentor, trainer and creative consultant.

Published by Peepal Tree Press, her debut collection, *Wild Cinnamon and Winter Skin* (2007), includes a poem, which was Highly Commended in the Forward Poetry Prize. *The Heart of It* (2012), her second collection, includes her poem "Operation Cast Lead" which was shortlisted in the Arvon International Poetry Competition (2010).

She has organised creative events and facilitated creative writing workshops and residences in schools, colleges and community settings, working across a range of abilities (from people with basic literacy skills to MA students) and with people from a variety of experiences and backgrounds.

She is particularly interested in the relationship between poetry and trauma and has presented her paper, *Speaking the Unspeakable through Poetry: The Search for a Place of Healing and Witness after Trauma* at conferences in UK, US, South Africa and Kuwait.

She is a fellow of the Complete Works programme for diversity and quality in British Poetry and has collaborated with film-makers, visual artists, musicians and digital artists. In 2012 she was the poet in residence at the Ilkley Literature Festival and in 2013 she was commissioned by Aldeburgh Poetry Festival to create text in response Bill Jackson's photo graphic exhibition, *Dark Light.* In 2014 her film-poem, "Sitting for the Mistress" was shortlisted in the Southbank Film Poem competition. In 2016 she received an Arts Council grant to fund a collaboration with digital artist Shirley Harris to create a multi-media production, *Lady of Situations*, which was launched at Off the Shelf Literature Festival, 2016. The work, which combined theatre, poetry, digital art and music, drew on the classical stories of Philomela and Tiresias and explored themes of power and control, gender identity, language and silence, trauma and recovery, exile, asylum and containment.

In 2018 she was selected as one of ten commissioned writers on the Colonial Countryside Project: National Trust Houses Reinterpreted. This is a child-led writing and history project with the University of Leicester, Peepal Tree Press and the National Trust.

www.seniseneviratne.com

ALSO BY SENI SENEVIRATNE

Wild Cinnamon and Winter Skin
ISBN: 9781845230500; pp. 64; pub. 2007; £7.99

Seni Seneviratne's debut collection offers a poetic landscape that echoes themes of migration, family, love and loss and reflects her personal journey as a woman of Sri Lankan and English heritage. The poems cross oceans and centuries. In "Cinnamon Roots", Seni Seneviratne travels from colonial Britain to Ceylon in the 15th century and back to Yorkshire in the 20th Century; in "A Wider View" time collapses and carries her from a 21st century Leeds back to the flax mills of the 19th century; poems like "Grandad's Insulin", based on childhood memories, place her in 1950s' Yorkshire but echo links with her Sri Lankan heritage.

"Loss, love, memory, from Yorkshire to Sri Lanka and back, Seni Seneviratne's poems delve in and out of a complex history. These tender, moving poems weave a delicate web." – Jackie Kay

"There's something about us. There are historians that may record our experiences. And these experiences may be found in the galleries of the future. Preserved. But it's in the poetry where the exhibits actually live. And it's here. Let Seni walk you through the labyrinthine gallery of wild cinnamon and winter skin." – Lemn Sissay

"Seni Seneviratne's poetry straddles continents and centuries – and does so with an easy fluency. The reader is drawn into her journey of discovery for her 'cinnamon roots' and her exploration of issues of identity and relationships. Personal and universal histories inter-weave in these poems." – Debjani Chatterjee

The Heart of It
ISBN: 9781845231903; pp. 64; pub. 2012; £8.99

Poet Mimi Khalvati writes:

"The movement of Seni Seneviratne's second collection, *The Heart of It*, is two-fold, like that of the heart: here is a poet able to combine the personal in enchanting lyrics of desire with the political in poems that, through imaginative power, portray other lives – marginalised, brutalised, lost – as genuinely as her own. Seni speaks to us in a voice always natural, engaging, never pushing beyond the limits of authentic feeling but staying true to lived experience and, despite loss or heartache, always open to the outside world and its windows on the heart. *The Heart of It* is a tender, moving collection, full of passionate intensity and an unswerving faith in the power of reconciliation and love."